Change Your Thoughts, Change Your Life Life Coach Manual

by Dr. Taketa Williams

ISBN 978-0-9825689-2-7

Website: www.taketawilliamsministries.org

Published by Exousia Book Publishing

7422 Atlantic Boulevard
Jacksonville, FL 32211 1-888-424-9673
Website: www.exousiabookpublishing.com

Scripture quotations are used primarily from the King James Version of the Bible, however a few other translations are used from various Bible versions.

Contents

Diary

Other Resources

Change Your Thoughts, Change Your Life
LIFE COACH MANUAL

Introduction

Our minds play a very important role in helping to bring about the success that God intends for us to have. God makes Joshua a promise in Joshua 1:8 and the promise is this, "This Book of the Law shall not depart from your mouth, but you shall meditate in it day and night, that you may observe to do according to all that is written in it. For then you will make your way prosperous, and then you will have good success" – NKJV. The requirement for success was that Joshua had to keep the Word in his mouth and mediate on the Word day and night. Meditation happens in the realm of the mind and means to imagine until our imagination becomes our actualization.

Before anything can exist in the natural realm it first has to pre-exist in the spiritual then the mental realm. The mental realm is a portal between heaven and earth that passes down the will of God into our lives. When God wants to reveal His will to mankind often times He will do so through visions and dreams. Visions and dreams are typically conferred from God who is in Heaven, downloaded into our minds, spoken out of our mouths, and ultimately manifested on earth. Dreams do come true, however they must first be embraced as truth in the mind. Whatever life our mind can believe determines the outcome we receive.

The successful life we desire to achieve must first be conceived in our thought life before it can be received. The mind is like a fertile womb and must be infiltrated with good seed in order to produce good ideas and good results. The womb of the mind has the potential to immediately get pregnant with a thought that will ultimately help or hinder our future success. Positive thoughts will produce positive outcomes and negative thoughts will give birth to negative circumstances. In essence, we create our success or failure through the thoughts we think. Whatever we think we can have, we will have. Whatever we think we can do, we will do. Whatever we think we can be, we will be. We are exactly what we think. Our thoughts determine who we are, what we will do, and what we will be. The summation of the value of man is determined by the sum total of his thoughts. A man's net worth is not measured alone by his money and assets, but vastly by his ability to think profitable thoughts and rewarding ideas.

We have been given the power to create the life we desire, a life by design. A life that is custom made and a designer's original. We are only several thoughts away from experiencing a brand new life and recreating a fresh new world. As we change our thoughts, we will change our life. Think about who you want to be, where you want to be, and what you desire to have. Let's allow our minds to become an incubation place for premature ideas to grow and be formed into full manifestations. As time progresses, our minds will nurture our thoughts until the underdeveloped intangible is fully developed into tangible things.

Let the coaching begin! Game day awaits you! You are destined to win!

About the Author

Dr. Taketa Williams is a highly anointed, vibrant, and powerful prophet called to the Nation and the Nations. She travels extensively all over the US and her ministry graces international territories. She is known as the "Preachers Preacher." The minis-try that God has placed inside of her is dynamic and the capacity in which He uses her will knock you off your feet! When she goes forth, lives are changed, bound men and women are set free, and the glory and the manifestation of God's presence is revealed! She touches lives all over the world and ministers to millions through her television ministry called "Ex-ousia," aired on the Word Network – the number one television source for urban ministries.

She co-pastors the Impact Christian Center alongside her husband, Apostle Roderick A. Williams. They have a cutting edge ministry established on four core values: Excellence, Education, Evangelism and Etiquette. Ultimately, the Impact Christian Center serves as a deliverance center, dream center and destiny center that assist individuals in walking in their deliverance, fulfilling their purpose, and reaching their destiny.

Dr. Williams is also the CEO of PTW Ministries, a global outreach ministry with a mandate to carry the Spirit of Revival to the nation and the nations. Her ministry has frequented the pulpits of great people of God globally. Her ministry also holds dynamic glory encounters each year such as: The B.A.D. (Bold, Anointed and Dynamic) Summit and the Glory Summit where people come to be shifted into new realms of life and Godliness.

Amongst her many accomplishments, Dr. Williams is the author of the books "50 Days Until Revival, My Cup Runs Over, and Scriptures For Everyday Living, I Can See Clearly Now and the Re-Defined You". In addition, Dr. Williams is an establishmentarian and has formed and developed schools and classes such as the

Impact Preachers Institute, PTW Ministries Biblical Institute of Technology, The Prophetic School of Ministry, The School of Esther and Kingdom Economics.

Her successes are ongoing and innumerable. In 2009, she launched a fragrance and skin care line called Successations. During a 21- day fast at the beginning of the year, God gave her 7 keys to walking through the door of opportunity. The seventh key was that in order to go through the door, that one had to carry the scent of success and the fragrance of their future; hence Successations with the tagline "Success Smells Good on You." With fragrances such as Zoe, Shaba, Destiny, Success and Divine Acceleration, the line follows the pattern of the life of Queen Esther who purified herself "on purpose" in fragrances for 12 months and at the opportune time engaged the king, disengaged her enemy and received as her reward half of the kingdom. The line includes body scrubs, balms, body butter, body oil, and candles. View her products online at http:// www.successations.com.

Set A New Record

The average person thinks about 60,000 thoughts per day. Approximately 45,000 of those thoughts are negative. Let's break the statistics and set a new record. Endeavor to think at least 60,000 positive thoughts today. Here are some things to think about.

"Summing it all up, friends, I'd say you'll do best by filling your minds and meditating on things true, noble, reputable, authentic, compelling, gracious--the best, not the worst; the beautiful, not the ugly; things to praise, not things to curse."
Philippians 4:8 MSG

Think Big

It's impossible to think big if little has a hold on you. Don't allow little to frustrate you and to get the best of you. Think big! When thinking BIG it will only require 3 letters of thought. BIG requires less thinking than LITTLE, which consists of 6 letters. Thinking about little will demand twice as much thought than big. It's easier to think big! You have power over little. Take authority over little and turn it into much.

"And he commanded the multitude to sit down on the grass, and took the five loaves, and the two fishes, and looking up to heaven, he blessed, and brake, and gave the loaves to his disciples, and the disciples to the multitude. And they did all eat, and were filled: and they took up of the fragments that remained twelve baskets full." Matthew 14:19-20

Remain Optimistic

During your thirst for success, you will often need to be rejuvenated. As you drink from the cup of refreshing, don't ever look at your glass as half empty, but only half full. Know that after you drink, your cup now has a new opportunity to be filled.

The Latin word for optimistic is optimum. To achieve optimum results and peak performance you must remain optimistic.

Choose to be optimistic. Optimists get paid more, are healthier, happier, live longer, and are better at dealing with uncertainty and change.

Recognize Opportunities

An opportunity is an appropriate or favorable time or occasion. It is a set time for favour to be released. Keep a mental alertness to detect an opportunity before it arrives. Sense its coming so that you can prepare to be ready to embrace it when it comes. Clear your mental agenda and cancel all future appointments with distracting thoughts for they will cause your opportunity to be missed.

"Opportunities are never lost; someone will take the one you miss." ~Author Unknown

Expect Favour To Be Released

Today the adversary and adversity shall not triumph over you because the favour of God is released upon you. You are surrounded by the favour of God. The Lord promises in His word according to Psalm 5:12 that He will bless the righteous and protect him with favour. You are protected from the hand of the enemy. The hand of the Lord is strong upon you and at work for you. Expect preferential treatment, gifts and surprises, raises and bonus', promotions and increases, and overflow and abundance. You are triumphant, walk in your favour.

"By this I know that thou favourest me,
because mine enemy doth not triumph over me."
Psalm 41:11

Increase Your Expectations

Expectation is when your anticipation catches up with the revelation of what God wants to do! Determine in your mind and declare with your mouth what God has purposed to do. Expect God to do something incredible today. He is an incredible God. Recall the promises of God to your mind like Jeremiah so that you may increase in hope (expectation). The more you expect Him to do, the more He will do. God is not average but superlative. He will exceed all of your expectations.

"This I recall to my mind, therefore I have hope."
Lamentations 3:21

Believe That God Will Do Exceeding Abundantly

God will do exceeding abundantly above all that you can ask or think according to the power that works in you. Be certain that the power of God is active and in full operation in you. Take your spiritual vitamins by reading the word of the Lord so that you may increase in mental power. God will do much more than you ask Him but only according to the power that works in you. This power is both spiritual and mental power. Remain mentally strong and avoid becoming emotionally drained. If your mental power stops working, then God won't do the exceeding and release the abundantly in your life.

"Now to Him Who, by (in consequence of) the [action of His] power that is at work within us,

is able to [carry out His purpose and] do superabundantly, far over and above all that we [dare] ask or think [infinitely beyond our highest prayers, desires, thoughts, hopes, or dreams] - Ephesians 3:20 AMP

Keep Your Eyes On The Goal

In your endeavor to win in life, facing hurdles are sometimes a part of the process. Hurdling is sprinting over small barriers. No hurdler focuses on the hurdles in a race but rather the goal. If you are visually captivated by your hurdles in life more than likely you will trip, fall and ultimately lose the race. Never look down, look ahead. Keep your eyes on the goal. Only glance at the hurdle rapidly enough to conquer it and expeditiously advance to your end so that you can win.

"I run straight toward the goal to win the prize that God's heavenly call offers in Christ Jesus."
Philippians 3:14 GWT

Think About Who You Want To Be

You are exactly what you think. Your thoughts determine who you are, what you will do, and what you will be. The summation of the value of man is determined by the sum total of his thoughts. A man's net worth is not measured alone by his money and assets, but vastly by his ability to think profitable thoughts and rewarding ideas. Think a new upgraded you into being. You are exactly what you think. It's what you think about you that will make the difference.

"Such as a man thinketh in his heart (mind), so is he... " Proverbs 23:7

Think Yourself Happy

No matter what obstacle you may face remain determined to be happy. Happiness starts as a state of mind and ends up producing a blessed life. A blessed person is a happy person and a happy person is a blessed person. Lack of happiness robs you of your blessing. When you sense your emotions going in the wrong direction, think yourself happy to direct them back on course. Think about things that bring you happiness so that happiness can be delivered to the door of your heart. Your thoughts are like the delivery guy. They will deliver you what you order (think about). Just make sure you open the door when your package arrives.

"I think myself happy, king Agrippa, because I shall answer for myself this day before thee touching all the things whereof I am accused of the Jews." Acts 26:2

Don't Let The Enemy Steal Your Joy

Joy and strength are interchangeable. When your joy is depleted then your strength is exhausted. Success requires both courage to pursue and strength to persevere. No extraordinary accomplishment can be achieved without perseverance. The enemy is a thief whose purpose is to steal, kill and destroy. He realizes that without joy, frustration becomes the inevitable. Wherever there is frustration there is also disappointment and discouragement. Disappointment causes us to miss divine appointments. Discouragement disconnects us from courage. Without courage we stop pursing and when we stop pursuing we fail to reach a successful end.

"Dear brothers and sisters, whenever trouble comes your way, let it be an opportunity for joy." – James 1:2 NLT

It's Impossible For You To Faint

Be strong in the Lord and in the power of His might. Wait on the Lord so that He may renew your strength. Then you will mount up with wings as eagles. You will run and not get weary and walk (progress) and not faint. If you faint in the day of adversity then thy strength is small. As your strength grows, it becomes virtually impossible for you to faint. You have eagles' wings. Don't be weary instead mount up in the wind. Use the wind to your advantage. Allow the wind to help you to soar and go higher than you've ever been before.

"But they that wait upon the LORD shall renew their strength; they shall mount up with wings as eagles; they shall run, and not be weary; and they shall walk, and not faint." - Isaiah 40:31

You're Too Blessed To Be Stressed

Recognize that stressing doesn't provoke blessings. You are blessed and have no reason to be stressed. Because you are blessed, you are guaranteed to receive your blessing. The blessing is already in you. Simply think it and speak it forth out of you. The blessing of the Lord maketh one rich and adds no sorrow to it. Declare that all is well and that every need is met. Embrace your blessing and put an end to stressing. Stand in the strength of who you are – you are indeed blessed. Everything about you is blessed. The fruit of your body is blessed. The very ground you walk on is blessed. "Blessed are your eyes, for they see: and your ears, for they hear.", Matthew 13:16. The blessings of the Lord shall come upon you and overtake you as you hearken unto the word of the Lord.

" And all these blessings shall come on thee, and overtake thee, if thou shalt hearken unto the voice of the LORD thy God." - Deuteronomy 28:2

Desire Success

Knowing that success is the will of God for your life, it's alright to desire success. Success is the favorable accomplishment of a goal or a prosperous achievement of an endeavor. In order to walk in success, you must first make an attempt. Don't allow the fear of failure keep you from trying. If you fall, get back up. At least you tried. If you lose, win next time.

"In order to succeed, your desire for success should be greater than your fear of failure." – Bill Cosby

Live A Defeat Proof Life

Defeat is actually a 5 stage process that happens over time. According to its meaning defeat consists of Frustration, Depravation, Prevention, Elimination, and finally Mutilation.

DEFEAT suggests…

- to Frustrate (which is to disappoint),
- to Deprive of something expected;
- to Prevent the success of;
- to lose a game and become Eliminated from the race;
- Latin root means to Mutilate.

The only way you can conquer defeat is to get on your feet and stand against frustration. When you overcome frustration, then you instantly defeat defeat. Depravation, prevention, elimination, and mutilation are halted and negated when you make a decision to remain free from frustration. When frustration departs, the others vanishes with it. You were born to win – so live a defeat proof life.

"You were born to win, but to be a winner
you must plan to win, prepare to win,
and expect to win." – Zig Ziglar

Rise Up and Conquer

God never intended for you to be defeated. His purpose is for you to conquer, overcome and subdue. A true conqueror is one who holds fast to the faith no matter what. Under any and all circumstances he relentlessly believes. He stands fully confident in the midst of the worst, not shaken neither moved, and thinks the best into being. The word Conqueror is derived from the Greek root word 'NIKE' meaning to have victory over the struggle. You are more than a conqueror and have victory over all struggles.

"Nay, in all these things we are more than conquerors through him that loved us."
Romans 8:37

Dream Big

When dreaming, don't be intimidated if your dream is much larger than you – it should be. Inside your dream is housed a ream. A ream is something that is very large in size and quantity. Your dream houses something enormous, huge and astronomical. They are filled with greatness and when your dream comes to pass that same greatness is erupts. Dreams are like time bombs waiting to explode. At the appointed time they will blow you up!

In an older form of English a ream means to make room, to open, to widen and to enlarge. Your dream will cause your territory to become enlarged so that you can walk in the fullness of everything that God has for you. Your dream will make room for you and open up the way for you to auspiciously advance. Learn from yesterday, dream today, and you'll succeed tomorrow.

"Sometimes dreams are so mind blowing they seem too good to be true."
- Prophetess Taketa Williams

"It seemed like a dream, too good to be true, when GOD returned Zion's exiles." - Psalm 126:1 MSG

Never Mind The Dream Stompers

At times dreams can be intimating to others and cause them to feel inferior. Not everyone around you will be able to handle and applaud your dream. Some people will literally hate you because you dare to dream. They will attempt to murder your ideas, throw machetes at your mind, and stomp on your soul so you are prohibited from seeing your dream come to pass. When people can't digest your dream, they will vomit on you. They will violently and forcefully send forth words of hatred, bitterness and jealously at your heart with the intent to kill your desires and cause your dream to die. When people begin to hate you for your dream, dream harder because it actually validates that the dream is from God and destined to come to pass.

"And Joseph dreamed a dream, and he told it his brethren: and they hated him yet the more." Genesis 37:5

Take Time To Go To Your Think Tank

A think tank is a place to dump out all negative, burdensome thoughts and meditate upon healthy, wholesome thoughts. It is the place that you create space in your mind to make room for the Lord to download fresh new ideas and grow dreams into realities. The think tank is also a birthing room. It's the place where the womb of your mind dilates, your mental cervix opens, your water of hope breaks, and you push forth nurtured thoughts into a living being.

"A thought is an unseen thing and thing is seen thought. Turn your thoughts into things." - Prophetess Taketa Williams

A thing is a thought and a statement; possessions and belongs. Therefore, our thoughts and our words release actual things into our lives. Those things, through the power of our thoughts, manifest as tangible possessions and belongings. Use your thoughts to work for you. According to Romans 8:28 the bible declares, *"And we know that all things work together for good to them that love God, to them who are the called according to his purpose."* When you think, you send your thoughts on assignment to bring about good in your life.

THINK TANK

DATE __________

PROBLEMS

____

____

____

SOLUTIONS

____

____

____

NEW IDEAS

____

____

____

Don't worry, be happy. To worry means to strangle.
Worry chokes the life out of you. It's a silent killer.
Take the time to breath and believe.

THINK TANK

DATE__________

PROBLEMS

SOLUTIONS

NEW IDEAS

Remember to empty out all negative, burdensome thoughts and only allow healthy, wholesome thoughts to operate in you.

THINK TANK

DATE ___________

PROBLEMS

____

____

____

SOLUTIONS

____

____

____

NEW IDEAS

____

____

____

Don't meditate on problems. Mentally create solutions. Why take time even thinking about a problem if you're not willing to acquire a solution to resolve the problem.

THINK TANK

DATE__________

PROBLEMS

____

____

____

SOLUTIONS

____

____

____

NEW IDEAS

____

____

____

Eliminate unnecessary weight. Don't ponder about anything.
To ponder is to put weight and heaviness on the mind.

THINK TANK

DATE ___________

PROBLEMS

____

____

____

SOLUTIONS

____

____

____

NEW IDEAS

____

____

____

*Don't worry, be happy. To worry means to strangle.
Worry chokes the life out of you. It's a silent killer.
Take the time to breath and believe.*

THINK TANK

DATE__________

PROBLEMS

____

____

____

SOLUTIONS

____

____

____

NEW IDEAS

____

____

____

Remember to empty out all negative, burdensome thoughts and only allow healthy, wholesome thoughts to operate in you.

THINK TANK

DATE __________

PROBLEMS

____

____

____

SOLUTIONS

____

____

____

NEW IDEAS

____

____

____

Don't meditate on problems. Mentally create solutions. Why take time even thinking about a problem if you're not willing to acquire a solution to resolve the problem.

THINK TANK

DATE__________

PROBLEMS

____

____

____

SOLUTIONS

____

____

____

NEW IDEAS

____

____

____

Eliminate unnecessary weight. Don't ponder about anything.
To ponder is to put weight and heaviness on the mind.

THINK TANK

DATE ___________

PROBLEMS

____

____

____

SOLUTIONS

____

____

____

NEW IDEAS

____

____

____

Don't worry, be happy. To worry means to strangle.
Worry chokes the life out of you. It's a silent killer.
Take the time to breath and believe.

THINK TANK

DATE__________

PROBLEMS

____

____

____

SOLUTIONS

____

____

____

NEW IDEAS

____

____

____

Remember to empty out all negative, burdensome thoughts and only allow healthy, wholesome thoughts to operate in you.

THINK TANK

DATE ___________

PROBLEMS

____

____

____

SOLUTIONS

____

____

____

NEW IDEAS

____

____

____

Don't meditate on problems. Mentally create solutions. Why take time even thinking about a problem if you're not willing to acquire a solution to resolve the problem.

THINK TANK

DATE__________

PROBLEMS

____

____

____

SOLUTIONS

____

____

____

NEW IDEAS

____

____

____

Eliminate unnecessary weight. Don't ponder about anything. To ponder is to put weight and heaviness on the mind.

USE YOUR IMAGINATION

What Did You Envision Today?

A vision is a clear mental picture of your future. It's not the past, it's not the present, but it is your future.

DATE ____________ TIME __________

____

____

____

____

____

____

____

____

"For the vision is yet for an appointed time, but at the end it shall speak, and not lie: though it tarry, wait for it; because it will surely come, it will not tarry." – Habakkuk 2:3

USE YOUR IMAGINATION

What Did You Envision Today?

A vision is a clear mental picture of your future. It's not the past, it's not the present, but it is your future.

DATE ____________ TIME __________

____

____

____

____

____

____

____

____

"For the vision is yet for an appointed time, but at the end it shall speak, and not lie: though it tarry, wait for it; because it will surely come, it will not tarry." – Habakkuk 2:3

USE YOUR IMAGINATION

What Did You Envision Today?

A vision is a clear mental picture of your future. It's not the past, it's not the present, but it is your future.

DATE ____________ TIME __________

____

____

____

____

____

____

____

____

"For the vision is yet for an appointed time, but at the end it shall speak, and not lie: though it tarry, wait for it; because it will surely come, it will not tarry." – Habakkuk 2:3

USE YOUR IMAGINATION

What Did You Envision Today?

A vision is a clear mental picture of your future. It's not the past, it's not the present, but it is your future.

DATE ____________ TIME __________

____

____

____

____

____

____

____

____

"For the vision is yet for an appointed time, but at the end it shall speak, and not lie: though it tarry, wait for it; because it will surely come, it will not tarry." – Habakkuk 2:3

USE YOUR IMAGINATION

What Did You Envision Today?

A vision is a clear mental picture of your future. It's not the past, it's not the present, but it is your future.

DATE ____________ TIME __________

____

____

____

____

____

____

____

____

"For the vision is yet for an appointed time, but at the end it shall speak, and not lie: though it tarry, wait for it; because it will surely come, it will not tarry." – Habakkuk 2:3

*U*SE YOUR IMAGINATION

What Did You Envision Today?

A vision is a clear mental picture of your future. It's not the past, it's not the present, but it is your future.

DATE ____________ TIME __________

____

____

____

____

____

____

____

____

"For the vision is yet for an appointed time, but at the end it shall speak, and not lie: though it tarry, wait for it; because it will surely come, it will not tarry." – Habakkuk 2:3

*U*SE YOUR IMAGINATION

What Did You Envision Today?

A vision is a clear mental picture of your future. It's not the past, it's not the present, but it is your future.

DATE ____________ TIME __________

____

____

____

____

____

____

____

____

"For the vision is yet for an appointed time, but at the end it shall speak, and not lie: though it tarry, wait for it; because it will surely come, it will not tarry." – Habakkuk 2:3

USE YOUR IMAGINATION

What Did You Envision Today?

A vision is a clear mental picture of your future. It's not the past, it's not the present, but it is your future.

DATE ____________ TIME __________

____

____

____

____

____

____

____

____

"For the vision is yet for an appointed time, but at the end it shall speak, and not lie: though it tarry, wait for it; because it will surely come, it will not tarry." – Habakkuk 2:3

USE YOUR IMAGINATION

What Did You Envision Today?

A vision is a clear mental picture of your future. It's not the past, it's not the present, but it is your future.

DATE ____________ TIME __________

____

____

____

____

____

____

____

____

"For the vision is yet for an appointed time, but at the end it shall speak, and not lie: though it tarry, wait for it; because it will surely come, it will not tarry." – Habakkuk 2:3

USE YOUR IMAGINATION

What Did You Envision Today?

A vision is a clear mental picture of your future. It's not the past, it's not the present, but it is your future.

DATE ____________ TIME __________

___

___

___

___

___

___

___

___

"For the vision is yet for an appointed time, but at the end it shall speak, and not lie: though it tarry, wait for it; because it will surely come, it will not tarry." – Habakkuk 2:3

*U*SE YOUR IMAGINATION

What Did You Envision Today?

A vision is a clear mental picture of your future. It's not the past, it's not the present, but it is your future.

DATE ____________ TIME __________

____

____

____

____

____

____

____

____

"For the vision is yet for an appointed time, but at the end it shall speak, and not lie: though it tarry, wait for it; because it will surely come, it will not tarry." – Habakkuk 2:3

TRACK YOUR DREAMS

Take note of your dreams. Write them down. Be as specific as possible. Imaginary, color, objects, people, and places are all extremely important and are very meaningful to gain a clear interpretation of your dream.

Write A Detailed
Description Of Your Dream.

Date ________ Time ________________

____

____

____

____

____

____

____

____

Pray over your dream to make certain that your dream is from God. Dreams that are not from God usually turn into nightmares.

TRACK YOUR DREAMS

Take note of your dreams. Write them down. Be as specific as possible. Imaginary, color, objects, people, and places are all extremely important and are very meaningful to gain a clear interpretation of your dream.

Write A Detailed Description Of Your Dream.

Date ________ Time ________________

____

____

____

____

____

____

____

____

Pray over your dream to make certain that your dream is from God. Dreams that are not from God usually turn into nightmares.

TRACK YOUR DREAMS

Take note of your dreams. Write them down. Be as specific as possible. Imaginary, color, objects, people, and places are all extremely important and are very meaningful to gain a clear interpretation of your dream.

Write A Detailed Description Of Your Dream.

Date ________ Time ________________

Pray over your dream to make certain that your dream is from God. Dreams that are not from God usually turn into nightmares.

TRACK YOUR DREAMS

Take note of your dreams. Write them down. Be as specific as possible. Imaginary, color, objects, people, and places are all extremely important and are very meaningful to gain a clear interpretation of your dream.

Write A Detailed
Description Of Your Dream.

Date ________ Time ________________

____

____

____

____

____

____

____

____

Pray over your dream to make certain that your dream is from God. Dreams that are not from God usually turn into nightmares.

TRACK YOUR DREAMS

Take note of your dreams. Write them down. Be as specific as possible. Imaginary, color, objects, people, and places are all extremely important and are very meaningful to gain a clear interpretation of your dream.

Write A Detailed
Description Of Your Dream.

Date ________ Time ________________

____

____

____

____

____

____

____

____

Pray over your dream to make certain that your dream is from God. Dreams that are not from God usually turn into nightmares.

OTHER BOOKS
BY DR. TAKETA WILLIAMS

WWW. TAKETAWILLIAMSMINISTRIES.ORG

23412799R00039

Made in the USA
Columbia, SC
10 August 2018